ISBN 978-0-428-15038-9
PIBN 11249848

English
Français
Deutsche
Italiano
Español
Português

www.forgottenbooks.com

Mythology Photography **Fiction**
Fishing Christianity **Art** Cooking
Essays Buddhism Freemasonry
Medicine **Biology** Music **Ancient
Egypt** Evolution Carpentry Physics
Dance Geology **Mathematics** Fitness
Shakespeare **Folklore** Yoga Marketing
Confidence Immortality Biographies
Poetry **Psychology** Witchcraft
Electronics Chemistry History **Law**
Accounting **Philosophy** Anthropology
Alchemy Drama Quantum Mechanics
Atheism Sexual Health **Ancient History**
Entrepreneurship Languages Sport
Paleontology Needlework Islam
Metaphysics Investment Archaeology
Parenting Statistics Criminology
Motivational

KARL ROSENFIELD — TWO BEAUTIES — M. M. CAHUZAC
(Below)   (Above)

A Message from Rosedale

ROSEDALE NURSERIES (S. G. HARRIS, Prop.) TARRYTOWN, N.Y.

special message for our friends. We have had joy at Rosedale. The joy of growing the finest trees and flowering plants which knowledge and love combined make possible.

Joy has been ours because of the pride we have taken in the enduring friendships which have come to us. Enduring because built upon a common love for Nature's beautiful things and upon a bond of faith and trust reposed in us by those who have been our customers. Nay, not merely customers, but joint workers together in the realm of floriculture.

AND NOW FOR THE MESSAGE. The time approaches when it is possible and perhaps even probable that ROSEDALE will pass from its present ownership. Beautiful Westchester County is being transformed by a network of splendid modern motor roads. One of these, the SAW MILL RIVER PARKWAY, will ultimately pass

Through the Heart of Rosedale

We must therefore look ahead. For the next two years we shall refrain from any expansion of our valuable holdings. We shall devote these two years to gradually disposing of our stocks of Peonies, Iris, Phlox, Roses, etc.

There can of course be no change in quality. That has been established for thirty years. Where our stocks are large,

We shall Reduce Former Prices to meet the coming situation

The discounts shown on page 5 will convince you that this is no idle message which we send you. It is a message of ROSEDALE quality at less than ROSEDALE prices.

During our thirty years at Rosedale, we have never attempted to sell the lowest priced goods. But we have attempted and we hope we have succeeded in selling the very finest quality trees and plants at prices so reasonable that many of our first customers are still with us.

We know that you have confidence in ROSEDALE products. We feel that you will be glad to avail yourself of this exceptional opportunity to secure them. While this is not in any way, shape or manner a Closing-Out Sale, it is a wonderful opportunity for you arising from the probable interference of Westchester County Parkways with our Rosedale property.

or FALL PLANTING

larity and none are more easily grown. They are seldom at-
tly hardy, requiring no covering in the severest weather. They
. rich, deep loam. They demand much moisture at blooming
ns will, therefore, last longer and be equally fine in other respects.
ent value than the Peony. The first cost is the only cost, and
>r many years. The foliage is rich and of beautiful deep green
:al even when out of flower, and few other flowers are so well
:e more massive color effect when planted in a border or in a
:eased during the past few years since the new improved varieties
color from cream and pure white through the various shades
troon, in all possible combinations of tint and form.

ble Places for Peonies

all situations, not only because of the splendor of their blooms but
not out of place in almost any location. Care should be taken,
reading roots of trees and shrubs which would rob them of nour-
1 trees at a distance is beneficial. Peonies make a very attrac-
:ially if planted alternately with phlox so that the season of
r. They are also very effective in large beds, either alone or
.dance of cut flowers only, they may be planted in the vegetable

ions for Peony Collections

1y purchasers believe that price depends on the quality. While
general far from the truth. Price is regulated largely by supply
nand will increase more rapidly in some cases than the supply, so
will be reduced to the common level. A good sample of this is
:s in cultivation today and still in great demand although intro-
qually good introduced today would be held at $100 per root.
:mand would be great and the price would drop very slowly,
the demand. This would take many years as the stock of the
rocess) and the demand increases as the variety becomes better
ty does not become popular by reason of high quality the de-
and the price will rapidly drop. The price of peonies now rated
ry slowly in the years to come, owing to the increasing demand.
varieties now sold at less than $1.00 which should be in every
:iva Maxima, not all as well known, but they come at different
ng together our collection of nearly 200 varieties, we have elim-
ot believe we now have a single variety unworthy of cultivation.
e choice of color, season of bloom and price. As to color and
make a selection to one's taste. And the price of each is given
sheet.

rood varieties, not too expensive. For the benefit of intending
f which one might be happy to own. While these lists are made
years, it is not infallible and would not be agreed to by all. But
would agree with us. While to amateurs some of the prices in
peony fans will agree that the prices will not be greatly reduced
:reasing demand, for every one of these is a gem.

List No. 2	List No. 3
Priced $1 to $2	Priced at $2 or more
WHITE	**WHITE**
he	Frances Willard
s Schroeder	Kelway's Glorious
:elway	Le Cygne
.mile Lemoine	Alsace Lorraine
: Dessert	
'acquin	**PINK**
lanc	Elwood Pleas
PINK	Eugene Verdier
	Henry Avery
1y	Jeannot
e Bigot	Lady Alexandra Duff
e Chas. Gombault	La France
ora	Mme. Jules Dessert
ne	Martha Bulloch
mile Galle	Milton Hill
emonier	Reine Hortense
rousse	Sarah Bernhardt
Guerin	Solange
ules Elie	Therese
tenee	Tourangelle
le	Walter Faxon
RED	**RED**
_Rousseau	Longfellow
	M~~~ C~~~~~~~

A Month *of* Peonies According to Color

Let us help you select early, midseason and late varieties, so as to give a month of white, a month of yellow, a month of light pink, a month of deep pink, a month of red or a month of purple.

In the following list of Peonies according to color, we have indicated by the letter "E"—early; "M"—midseason; and "L"—late varieties. These are still further differentiated,· very early, early midseason, late midseason, very late in the descriptions in the full alphabetical list.

The earliest to bloom are the Officinalis varieties, which begin blooming in this vicinity about May 20th, the season closing June 25th to July 4th with such varieties as Grandiflora, Madame de Galhau, Madame Emile Galle, Marie Lemoine, Purpurea Superba and others.

Double Varieties

WHITE

Alba Sulphurea (M)
Albatre (M)
Alsace-Lorraine (L)
Avalanche (M)
Baroness Schroeder (M)
Boule de Neige (E)
Couronne d'Or (L)
Festiva (L)
Festiva Maxima (M)
Frances Willard (L)
James Kelway (M)
Jubilee (M)
Kelway's Glorious (M)
La Fiancee (M)
La Lorraine (M)
La Rosiere (M)
La Tendresse (E)
Le Cygne (E)
Marcelle Dessert (M)
Marie Lemoine (L)
Marie Jacquin (M)
Mme. Crousse (L)
Mme. de Verneville (E)
Mme. Emile Lemoine (M)
Mons. Dupont (M)
Mrs. Edw. Harding (M)

BLUSH OR FLESH COLORS

Albert Crousse (L)
Alfred de Musset (L)
Asa Gray (M)

Aurore (L)
Carnea Elegans (Calot) (L)
Dorchester (L)
Elwood Pleas (L)
Eugenie Verdier (M)
Galathee (L)
Germaine Bigot (M)
Gismonda (L)
Grandiflora (L)
Henry Avery (M)
Jeannot (L)
Mlle. Leonie Calot (L)
Mlle. Marie Calot (L)
Mlle. Rousseau (M)
Mme. Auguste Dessert (M)
Mme. Calot (E)
Mme. de Galhau (M)
Mme. de Vatry (M)
Marguerite Gerard (M)
Marie Crousse (M)
Mary Woodbury Shaylor (M)
Milton Hill (L)
Number One (L)
Octavie Demay (E)
Pierre Duchartre (L)
Rosa Bonheur (M)
Solange (L)
Souv. de Louis Bigot (M)
Therese (E)
Tourangelle (M)
Triomphe de l'Exposition de Lille (M)

YELLOW

Dr. Bretonneau (Guerin) (M)
Duchess de Nemours (M)
Duke of Wellington (M)
Grandiflora Nivea Plena (E)
Laura Dessert (E)
Philomele (M)
Primevere (M)

MEDIUM PINK

Eugene Verdier (L)
Gloire de Charles Gombault (M)
Jeanne d'Arc (E)
Lady Alexandra Duff (E)
La France (L)
Lamartine (M)
Livingstone (L)
Mme. Bollet (M)
Mme. Ducel (E)
Mme. Emile Galle (L)
Mme. Jules Dessert (L)
Mme. Lemonier (M)
Martha Bulloch (L)
Mons. Jules Elie (E)
Reine Hortense (M)
Sarah Bernhardt (M)
Umbellata Rosea (E)
Venus (M)

DEEPER PINKS

Claire Dubois (L)
Edulis Superba (E)
General Bertrand (E)
Modeste (Guerin), (E)
Mons. Barral (L)
Mons. Boucharlat Aine (M)
Petite Renee (M)
Walter Faxon (M)

RED

Augustin d'Hour (M)
Eugene Bigot (M)
Felix Crousse (M)
Karl Rosenfield (E)
Longfellow (M)
Lord Kitchener (M)
Officinalis Rubra (E)
Rubra Superba (L)

DEEP RED AND PURPLE

Adolphe Rousseau (E)
Cherry Hill (E)
De Candolle (M)
Delachei (M)
Mme. Gaudichau (M)
Mons. Martin Cahuzac (E)
Prince de Talindyke (L)
Phillipe Rivoire (E)
Raphael (E)

Japanese and Single Peonies—(*Mostly Early to Midseason*)

WHITE

Eglantine (S)
Isani-Gidui (J)
La Fiancee (S)
Lemon Queen (J)
Lucienne (S)
Le Jour (S)
Marguerite Dessert (S)

WHITE

Queen of May (S)
Snow Wheel (J)
Whitleyi Major (S)
Yeso (J)
Rosy Dawn (S)

PINK

Emily (S)
Hermes (S)

PINK

Ama-No-Sode (J)
Clairette (S)
Madeline Gauthier (S)
Pride of Langport (S)
Tokio (J)
Venise (S)
Festiva Fragrans (S)
Tamatbako (J)

RED

Carnot (S)
Fuyajo
Darkness (S)
Kino-Kimo (J)
L'Etincelante (S)
Mikado (J)
Some Ganoko (J)
The Moor (S)
Veloutine (S)

For twenty-five years we have been interested in collecting and growing the best peonies. We have from time to time rejected varieties that did not come up to our high ideal, with the hope of reducing our list to 100 varieties. But many new varieties have come out in recent years, some of which are superior to many of the older varieties. Thus we have been adding as well as rejecting, and our list now comprises only the best varieties.

The Best Size Roots to Buy

While our strong 3-5 eye roots will nearly all bloom for you the first year if planted in September, the 1-year size is the best buy, being about double the size at the price of only about one-half more.

Read on Page 5 what Secretary Saunders says about divisions.

SPECIAL REMOVAL DISCOUNTS
Shown on Page 5
Make This a Golden Opportunity For You

If In Doubt, Ask Us

From the short descriptions in any peony list, the buyer is often at a loss to decide. We suggest, FIRST: Forget about prices; for many of the good ones are only $1.00 or less: (e. g.) Festiva Maxima at 75c is unexcelled by any other white peony priced at less than $5.00. SECOND: Note carefully the rating. If a variety is rated 8.0 or above, you cannot go wrong, no matter how low the price, and there are quite a number below 8.0 that should be in every collection. No peony lover could do without Edulis Superba 7.6, Gloire de Chas. Gombault 7.9, Mme. de Verneville 7.9, or Mme. Crousse and Mme. de Galhau 7.5. THIRD: Be sure to place your order with a reliable house, even though prices may be a little higher, and, where possible, order nothing less than one or two year plants, preferably the latter.

These Peony Discounts Will Interest You

On orders of not less than three plants of a kind and amounting to $10.00 to $50.00, we will make a discount of 15 per cent.; on orders of $50.00 and up, 20 per cent. On varieties priced at $2.00 and up prices are net. Write for special quotation on large orders.

No charge for boxing and packing. Discounts do not apply to special offer. The best discount we can give is Mrs. Harding's book, "Peonies in the Little Garden", with every order for $15 for Peonies and Iris.

It will be to your interest to order at once to secure the plants you wish. Some of the varieties will be sold out before planting time.

Special Offer ! To those wishing plants for mass planting, or cut-flowers, and not particular about names we offer a bargain. Strong 3 to 5 eye divisions, $2.50 per ten; $20.00 per 100. Strong 1-year clumps, $4.00 per ten; $35.00 per 100; 50 at 100 rate. 10 pink, white or red, divisions, 30 cents each; 50 or more at 25 cents each; 1-year, 45 cents each, 50 or more at 40 cents each.

If you could have had this special offer and seen our plants in bloom in June your order would be a large one.

IMPORTANT

Concerning the sizes of plants, Prof. Saunders well says: "I feel that I should not lay down my typewriter without saying a word regarding a new practice which has come into the Peony business of late years I refer to the selling of what are called 'divisions' or 'one-eye divisions,' 'two-eye divisions,' etc. What are called one-year roots are the plants that have resulted from the divisions of last year. But evidently the nurseryman can save himself money by selling the divisions at once to his customers, without taking the trouble to replant and cultivate for a year. These freshly made divisions are very commonly offered in the trade and at prices much below those for one-year roots. My own judgment on it is this: where the question of price has to be very carefully considered and the question of time is a matter of indifference, the buyer may probably do well to buy divisions of the expensive sorts. BUT WHAT HE SAVES IN MONEY HE LOSES IN TIME; FOR WHEREAS A ONE-YEAR ROOT WILL USUALLY BLOOM WELL WITHIN TWO OR THREE YEARS AFTER PLANTING, AND WILL GIVE SOME BLOOM EVEN THE FIRST YEAR, A DIVISION CANNOT BE EXPECTED TO GIVE GOOD BLOOM FOR A CONSIDERABLY LONGER TIME. * * * But no one need spend a great deal of money in order to have a beautiful collection of Peonies, provided he is willing to confine himself to the older sorts. Those who must have the novelties cannot do better than take counsel with others who have tried the experiment of small divisions before committing themselves too far."

Much might be added to what Prof. Saunders says about these small divisions. Mrs. Harding has well covered the case in her little book about Peonies which we are offering as a prize and we sincerely hope buyers will take heed of what these good authorities say and that the custom of selling small divisions will be done away. These small divisions in the high priced varieties may be worth while by experts, but for the amateur, it would seem to me ill-advised to purchase anything less than the 3-5 eye divisions.

We wish prospective customers could see our fine fields of one year plants grown strong and husky from 3-5 eye divisions planted last Fall. Although we have taken pains to plant and care for these roots a whole year, giving them time to make a year's growth and heal all bruises and cuts, nevertheless- we are offering these plants at prices lower than divisions are offered in some quarters, in accordance with our motto, "Prices as low as consistent with highest quality."

net and amaranth, very brilliant................

8.1 **Asa Gray.** (Crousse, 1886). Pale lilac sprinkled with dots of deeper lilac. Large, rose shape; very fragrant; medium height and habit. Midseason.......... 1.00

7.8 **Augustin d'Hour.** (Calot, 1867). Dark, brilliant rose-red. Medium to large, bomb-shape; showy bloom; medium height. Midseason. (Similar in color to Felix Crousse) .... .75

8.0 **Aurore.** (Dessert, 1904). Blush, lighter collar, slightly flecked with crimson. Large, flat, loose; medium height; compact bush. Late......................... .75

8.7 **Avalanche.** (Crousse, 1886). Creamy-white, slightly flecked with carmine. Large, compact, crown type; fragrant; strong growth. Nothing better. Often sold under name of Albatre. Midseason..................................... .75

9.0 **Baroness Schroeder.** (Kelway 1889). Flesh, fading to milk-white. Large globular, rose type; strong free bloomer. One of the best standard kinds. Late midseason.. 1.00

8.0 **Boule de Neige.** (Calot, 1867). Milk-white, flecked with crimson. Very large, regular and compact; tall, erect growth. Early............................ .50

7.0 **Canari.** (Guerin, 1861). Guards amber-white, tinted pink; center clear yellow, fragrance X. Late... .50

7.8 **Carnea Elegans.** (Calot, 1860). Soft flesh color flecked with crimson. Large, flat, compact, rose type; fragrant; medium height, late. Professor Saunders well says: "indoors they preserve an enchanting combination of flesh color and pale yellow." .... .75

8.6 **Cherry Hill.** Semi-rose type. Deep garnet, decided sheen. Tall and erect. Midseason 3.50

8.7 **Claire Dubois.** (Crousse, 1886). Even, clear, satiny pink, tipped white. Very large, globular rose type; tall, erect, strong growth. Very late................. 1.00

8.1 **Couronne d'Or.** (Calot, 1873). White with yellow tints arising from a few stamens showing amidst the petals. Center petals tipped with carmine. Large, rather full flower of superb form. Strong grower and very free bloomer. Good keeper. Late... .75

7.2 **De Candolle.** (Crousse, 1880). Uniform bright lilac-purple; beautiful under artificial light. Very large, full, rose type; medium height; strong erect grower. Late midseason .... .50

7.1 **Delachei.** (Delache, 1856). Violet-crimson. Medium size; semi-rose type; strong, erect, vigorous growth. Midseason to late.............................. .75

6.9 **Docteur Bretonneau.** (Guerin, 1850). Guards flesh-pink, center yellow, sometimes salmon. Midseason .... .50

7.7 **Dorchester.** Delicate shade of hydrangea pink, compact rose type. Very late.... .75

7.8 **Duc de Wellington.** (Calot, 1859). Pure white guards. sulphur center. Large, bomb-shape; very fragrant; tall, erect growth. Midseason.............. .50

In comparing prices with those of other growers, please note that we offer strong one and plants, and large divisions, 3-5 eye. These one year plants have grown from strong divisions year ago, which has given time to heal the callouses and produce plenty of fibrous roots. plants are much more valuable than divisions goes without saying.

	3-5 eye	1 yr.	2 yr.
(Calot, 1856). Guard petals white, center lemon-yellow, cup-st; it develops into a large bloom, gradually fading to white; ong grower and free bloomer. Extra good commercial variety. to three days later than Festiva Maxima....................	.50	.75	
noine, 1824). Dark pink, even color; large, loose, crown when Very fragrant; upright growth, early bloomer. One of the best >eonies. There is much confusion over this variety being sold · or more different names..................................	.50	.75	1.25
s, 1900). Very soft, shell pink; compact flower of rose type. :r, free bloomer. Large, fragrant and beautiful. Late........	2.50	3.00	
sert, 1894). Brilliant red, medium size, compact, globular, pe. Free bloomer. Midseason...........................	1.50	2.00	
ot, 1864). Light pink with lilac-white collar. Large, rose type; growing plant; erect, rather dwarf. Fragrant. Awarded first an Peony Show 1923 for six specimen blooms, named, one e. Be sure you get the real thing; it is one of the best........	1.50	2.00	3.00
ilot, 1864). (Also called Pottsi Alba). Pale pink, center deep-·imson. Large flat, rose type, rather loose; fragrant; tall, free.	1.00		
usse, 1881). Very brilliant red. Medium to large, globular, > shape; fragrant; strong growth. Midseason................	.75	1.00	1.50
, 1838). Pure paper white with crimson markings in center. very fragrant; dwarf. Late....................	.50	.75	1.00
Aiellez, 1851). Paper-white with crimson markings in center. ind full, rose type; very tall, strong growth. The best early ; very fragrant...............................	.50	.75	1.25
Jrand, 1907). Blush white with occasional carmine blotch and pure white. Large perfectly formed flower of semi-rose type. er; free bloomer, on strong, erect stems; quite fragrant. Late	1.50	2.00	-
1900). Flesh white. Large, full rose type. Strong grower; t and very late. One of the best...........................	3.00	3.50	
[Guerin, 1846). Dark pink, silvery center. Large anemone n, with broad collar; fragrance XX; tall, strong, upright growth.	.50	.75	1.00
essert, 1902). Flesh pink, salmon tints; center flecked crimson. flower, rose type. This is one of Dessert's excellent varieties. we imported it from him, 15 years ago, we have thought very . It is not only beautiful in color, but its large blooms are at profusion, standing up well on strong stems. Excellent mid-ety	.75	1.25	2.00
This is a very good fragrant Peony; blooms are flesh colored, ose in the center. Very late...............................	1.00	1.50	2.00
mbault. (Dessert, 1896). Guard petals fleshy-pink, collar clear shaded with apricot; center petals flesh-pink, striped with owers very showy, on tall stems in great profusion; crown type. son	1.00	1.50	2.00
rdson, 1883). Beautiful flesh-pink, with lighter shades at the of the very largest pinks known. Vigorous, fragrant. One of > bloom.	.75	1.00	2.00
na. (Lemoine, 1824). Guard petals pure white, center slightly ur and pink, and flecked with crimson. Very large, rose type; igrant. Very early...........................	.50	.75	1.00
i petals and center, light flesh pink; collar clear bright yellow. Midseason...................................	3.00	3.50	
lway, 1900). Rosy white changing to milk white. Very large, pe; fragrant; tall, strong. Early midseason................	1.00	1.50	2.25
t, 1858). Soft pink guard; collar rich cream and bright pink r, tipped carmine. Medium to large, crown shape; fragrant; :r, free bloomer. Early midseason. One of the choicest of older each-blossom pink and cream, reminds one of peaches and ly	.75	1.00	1.50
slightly tinged purple. Large cup-shaped flowers. Late......	5.00	6.00	
'8). Color flesh white, fading to pure white. Petals narrow, inged, giving a feathery effect. Long stems. Strong grower. r. Fragrant. Midseason.................................	1.50	2.00	3.00
osenfield, 1908). Brilliant deep crimson. Very strong, com-and free bloomer. One of the best. Semi-rose type; excellent ly midseason..................................	.75	1.00	1.50
(Kelway, 1909). Creamy-white, with a soft blush of pink. ooms of rose type; very fragrant. Generally considered one of it. Late midseason....................................	8.00	10.00	

			1 yr.	2 yr.

9.1 Lady Alexandra Duff. (Kelway, 1902). Outer petals delicate pink, gradually shading lighter toward center. An immense cup-shape flower; broad, imbricated petals, large and full in old plants. In young plants and the side buds of older plants, blooms are water lily shape, showing yellow stamens at center. Fragrant, tall and robust. One of Kelway's best. True variety from Shaylor. Early .... 2.00   2.50   [3-5 eye]

7.5 La Fiancee. (Lemoine, 1901). Large blooms of creamy white, sometimes flecked with crimson in center, bomb type. Midseason............... .... .75

9.0 La France. (Lemoine, 1901). Soft pink outer guards, splashed crimson. Very large, compact flower of rose type. Strong grower, free bloomer, very fragrant. Very late................................ 3.00   4.00

8.6 La Lorraine. (Lemoine, 1901). Creamy white with a faint salmon pink tinge; very large, globular flower. Late midseason............................ 5.00

8.3 Lamartine. (Calot, 1860). (Also called G'gantea). Pale lilac-rose, darker center. Very large, loose, irregular, rose shape; tall, free bloomer; very fragrant. Early midseason.................................. .75   1.50   2.25

8.5 La Perle. (Crousse, 1886). Lilac white, blush center, flecked with crimson. Very large, globular flower; rose type, fragrant. Midseason.................. 1.00

8.3 La Rosiere. (Crousse, 1888). Pure white shading to cream in center, due to presence of yellow stamens. Large, flat, semi-double; medium height. Name is well chosen for its strong fragrance. Midseason. American Peony Society award 1923, for twenty blooms, double, named, white or cream........ .75   1.00

8.1 La Tendresse. (Crousse, 1896). Cream color, changing to pure white, slightly splashed carmine; rose type; very large, compact, flat; fragrant. Strong, upright growth. Early midseason.................................... .75   1.00   1.50

8.8 Laura Dessert. (Dessert, 1913). Guards, cream white; center, bright canary yellow. Large, full flower; rose type; superb. Early. Like other yellow peonies, it should be opened in the house to retain its rich yellow........ 4.00

9.9. Le Cygne. (Lemoine, 1907). Milk white flower. Petals incurved. Perfectly formed, enormous globular flower. Very fragrant. Early............... 7.00   9.00

8.1 Livingstone. (Crousse, 1879). Soft rose pink, silver tipped, some carmine spots. Large, compact, rose type; tall, vigorous, free bloomer. Very late........ .75   1.00

9.0 Longfellow. (Brand, 1907). Bright crimson with cherry tone; perhaps the most brilliant of red peonies. Erect habit, vivid color, long season, rare value. Originator says, "It is the most brilliant peony in our whole list." Midseason 2.50   3.50

7.8 Lord Kitchener. Bright cherry red. Large bomb type flowers. Midseason........ 1.50

8.6 Mme. Auguste Dessert. (Dessert, 1899). Glossy flesh, slightly tinged carmine; center flecked crimson. Very large, imbricated, cup-shaped flower, rose type; erect; medium height. Early midseason.............................. 1.00   1.50

7.4 Mme. Bollet. (Calot, 1867). Pale lilac-pink, silvery reflex. Large, very compact, rose type; upright growth. Late midseason........................... .50   .75   1.00

7.3 Mme. Bucquet. (Dessert, 1888). Dark crimson amaranth. Semi-double flowers; strong grower. Midseason...................................... .75   1.00   1.50

8.1 Mme. Calot. (Miellez, 1856). Flesh white, tinged pale hydrangea pink, center shaded slightly darker with a sulphur tint; very large, full, globular bloom; fragrant; early and abundant bloomer. On well established plants the flowers are exquisite .... .50   .75   1.00

6.8 Mme. Chaumy. Pale lilac rose with silvery reflex. Large globular flowers; rose shaped. Late .... .50   .75   1.00

7.9 Mme. Crousse. (Calot, 1866). Pure white with faint crimson markings. Large, globular, crown type; fragrant; medium height. Late midseason.......... .50   .75   1.00

7.5 Mme. de Galhau. (Crousse, 1883). Delicate pink with a rose-white collar. Very large, compact, rose shape; very fragrant; strong growth. Very late...... .50   .75   1.00

7.7 Mme. de Vatry. (Guerin, 1863). Pink guards, high cream-color center, very large, full, crown-shaped. Late .... .50   .75   1.00

7.9 Mme. de Verneville. (Crousse, 1885). Pure white, center tipped with carmine, very large, full bomb shape, fragrant, medium height, strong growth, very early .... .50   .75   1.00

7.9 Mme. Ducel. (Mechin, 1880). Bright silvery pink. Very large, well built flower; bomb type; strong grower; free bloomer; odor pleasant; medium height; one of the best. Early midseason .... .50   1.00   1.50

8.5 Mme. Emile Galle. (Crousse, 1881). Very soft pink, changing to milk-white in center. Very large, compact, flat, rose type; tall, fragrant. Late.......... 1.00   1.50

8.9 Mme. Emile Lemoine. (Lemoine, 1899). Glossy white, tinged pale pink and covered with tiny dots of deeper shade. Large, globular, rose type; a strong grower, good bloomer. One of the best. Midseason............................ 1.00   1.50

8.5 Mme. Gaudichau. Very dark maroon. Foliage dark red when first appearing. Midseason 2.50   3.50

9.4 Mme. Jules Dessert. (Dessert, 1909). Clear pink, tinged flesh and straw yellow, undulated central petals, flecked with carmine and intermixed with a few visible golden stamens. Very large, imbricated flower of fine shape; one of the most beautiful in color and form. When the flower opens under cloudy weather, or in the house, the exquisite tints are really marvelous. Only four peonies rank higher than this. Late midseason. Price has increased with the great demand during the past three years......................... 2.00   3.00

Mme. Lemonier. (Calot, 1860). Exquisite pale pink. Very large globular bloom, rose type; strong grower and very free bloomer. "The size of this peony, its great height, robust habit and fine color, make it a most striking garden subject." Midseason. Much superior to Mme. Lemoinier, 1865, which is ranked at 8.0 .... .75   1.00   1.50

	3-5 eye	1 yr.	2 yr.
ert, 1909). Rose-carmine, large and full. Free flowering...	.75		1.25
alot, 1861). Very delicate shell-pink, center darker. Medium)act, globular. Late midseason. Its only fault a rather weak	.75	1.00	1.50
alot, 1872). Milk-white tinged flesh, flecked crimson. Large, / fragrant; strong grower. Late midseason	.50	.75	1.00
isse, 1886). Milk-white, splashed carmine. Large globular, a strong stem; medium height. Late midseason	.75		1.50
issert, 1899). Milk-white, slightly splashed with lilac; high d crimson. Fragrance of a tea rose. Midseason	1.00	1.50	2.00
rousse, 1892). Very pale salmon-pink, fading to almost white. t, rose type; very strong growth. Free bloomer. Late mid-	.75	1.00	1.50
ise, 1892). Soft salmon-pink. Large, full flower; bomb type; stems; very fragrant; tall, strong. Midseason	1.00	1.50	2.00
er). (Syn. Water Lily). Rose-white, fading to white. Large, double; upright, very strong growth; cup-shaped like a water)n	.75	1.00	1.50
t, 1869). Pure white with cream-white center. Large, very type; pleasing fragrance; medium height, extra strong stems. it; no collection is complete without it. Very late	.75	1.00	1.50
ld, 1907). Soft rose pink. Enormous cup-shaped flower. One ionies in existence and exquisitely beautiful. Strong grower. Fragrant. Late	5.00	6.00	
or. (Shaylor, 1916). The guard petals of the flower are fresh the center a creamy yellow. Plant of dwarf growth with stiff irofuse bloomer	5.00	6.00	
lson). Soft, clear, flesh color, deepening toward the center. iis flower a quality of color that is beyond the power of words Very large globular, compact, rose type; fragrant. Very late.	3.00	4.00	5.00
irin, 1845). Very attractive, bright pink, tinged carmine, solid iloom, typical bomb type; fragrance XX. Fine upright habit, , early and free. We consider this the best carmine-pink peony. fhe American Beauty Peony	.75		
it, 1872). Milk-white, center splashed with crimson. Large emi-rose type; fragrant; tall, erect. Late midseason	.75		
ousse, 1888). Pale lilac-rose, silvery reflex. Very large, com- ; very fragrant; tall, vigorous growth. Early	1.00	1.50	2.00
. (Dessert, 1899). Very dark garnet with black reflex, petals o appear varnished. Medium to large, globular, semi-rose type. .t; strong, vigorous grower. Early midseason	2.00	2.50	
. Pure white flower. Semi-rose type. Late midseason	12.00		
id, imported variety; exquisite shell pink flower of large size form; center splashed with crimson after the manner of Festiva se type; very late. It excels in attractiveness many of the l peonies. A royal variety; greatly admired by all who see it..	1.00	1.50	2.25
ot, 1867). Pale pink, collar almost white with a few stripes of ·y large, flat, crown type; fragrant; dwarf plant with strong, Early	.75	1.00	1.50
uble crimson, of large size; fragrant; the old-fashioned red y.	.75	1.00	1.50
361). Yellow, fading to cream, with bright pink guards and m size; low, flat crown; medium height; strong growth; fra- ison	.75	1.00	1.50
it, 1899). Dark pink. Very large, anemone shape, semi-double ke center petals. Medium height, upright. Midseason	1.00	1.50	2.25
oire, 1911). This is one of the finest red Peonies. Of excellent ir this Peony has the fragrance of a tea rose. Strong grower mer. Midseason	7.50		
iin, 1890). Dark red shaded garnet. Semi-rose type. Early..		1.00	
ousse, 1895). Flesh-pink. Very full, cup-shaped flower, rose rect, strong grower. Very late	.75	1.00	
1907). Outer petals buff, center sulphur yellow. Tall, strong, ree bloomer. Very fragrant. Midseason	2.00	3.00	4.00
Dark purple. Large; distinct. Winner of the first prize at ican Peony Society Exhibition, June, 1910, for fifty best blooms, ties. Stems erect and vigorous; nearly four feet tall. Late....	.75	1.00	
iert, 1910). Clear mauve shaded carmine pink; very full, big ect shape; free bloomer; a variety of great beauty, in great de- rant	5.00	6.00	
382). Dark purple garnet, medium size globular center; rose erect grower. Very early	.75	1.00	
lot, 1857). (Syn. President Taft). Light shell pink, center on; very striking; large, well formed flowers, semi-rose type, igrant. Midseason	1.00	1.50	2.00
and). Red, large globular bomb type. Guard petals broad t; center gathered in an immense central dome. Delicate fra- of the earliest to bloom	3.00	4.00	

9.7 **Solange.** (Lemoine, 1907). The outer petals are very delicate lilac white, deepening toward the center with salmon shading; center deep orange salmon. A very large, full, compact flower of rose type; strong grower and free bloomer; delightfully fragrant. Very late. No better peony exists. Awarded first prize at American Peony Show 1923 for one specimen bloom, double, any variety, representing the best bloom at the Show; was as good the last day as when the judges passed upon it...................................... 2.50   3.50

9.1 **Souv. de Louis Bigot.** (Dessert, 1913). Rich salmon pink with silvery lights. Very large blooms, extra fine, late midseason. Mrs. Harding says it is a real treasure. Its effect in the garden is nothing short of gorgeous........... 3.50   4.50

9.8 **Therese.** (Dessert, 1904). Glossy flesh, lightly shaded pink, lighter at the center. Very attractive imbricated flowers, very large; rose type; one of the most beautiful flowers in color and form; very scarce. Early................. 2.50   3.00   4.50

9.4 **Tourangelle.** (Dessert, 1910). Flesh-pink, tinged with salmon; very delicate shade. Large flat flower of rose type, strong grower; free bloomer; very fragrant; superb. Midseason 2.00   2.50

7.8 **Triomphe de l'Exposition de Lille.** (Calot, 1865). Light shell pink, splashed with a darker tint. Large, compact, rose type; pleasing fragrance; strong growth. Midseason. Beautiful to the last.. .50   .75   1.25

7.1 **Umbellata rosea.** (Dessert, 1895). Violet-rose guards with amber-white center. Informal rose type; medium height; very strong; upright. Very early....... .50   .75

8.3 **Venus.** (Kelway). Very delicate, shell pink, lighter collar. Very large, high compact crown; rose fragrance; tall, erect. Midseason..................... .75   1.00

7.1 **Ville de Nancy.** (Calot, 1872). Brilliant red; very large, bomb shape, very strong grower. Late .... .50   .75

9.3 **Walter Faxon.** (Richardson). Coral salmon pink; very distinct delicate color, deepening toward the center; semi-rose type. Strong grower and free bloomer. Midseason 3.00   4.00

SINGLE AND JAPANESE PEONIES

9.2 **Ama-no-sode.** (Japan). Bright Rose Pink, shading lighter to the edge. Superb.... 8.00   10.00

Carnot. (Dessert). Single, red. Early........................... 1.00   1.50

8.5 **Clairette.** (Dessert, 1905). A superb, large white, lightly shaded pink, changing to pure white 2.00   2.50

7.1 **Darkness.** Single. Very dark maroon surrounding cluster of golden stamens....... 1.00   1.50

8.1 **Eglantine.** (Dessert, 1913). Large, white, single flower, slightly tinted carmine, central tuft of golden stamens. Superb variety, like a gigantic Eglantine rose 2.00   3.00

7.4 **Emily.** Soft rose pink.. 1.00   1.50

Festiva Fragrans. Clear single pink.. .75   1.50

9.2 **Fuyajo.** (Japan). Guard petals deep red with dark crimson petaloids in center.... 6.00   7.00

Hermes. Single. Soft shade of deep shell pink............................... .50   .75

9.3 **Isani-Gidui.** (Japan). Very large, pure white, single flower, with silky broad petals, big central tuft of golden yellow stamens or filamentous petals; strong grower and free bloomer. A splendid variety of marvelous beauty. One grower is asking $25 for a one-eye root.............................. 8.00   10.00

8.2 **Kino-Kimo.** (Japan). Crimson-carmine; large central tuft of filamentous petals, golden yellow, streaked with carmine................................... 1.50   2.00

8.4 **La Fiancee.** (Dessert, 1902). (Syn.—The Bride). Very large, single, white with yellow center. Early. Good variety. Carpels greenish-white and hairy; stigmas long, white and recurved. Odor slight. Plant is strong, coarse grower, with a very spreading habit. Free bloomer. Characteristic coarse, thick, leathery foliage; a third larger bloom than the ordinary albiflora...... 1.75   2.25

8.6 **Le Jour.** Single. Very large white of extra quality........................... 3.50   4.50

Lemon Queen. (Japan). Pure white with central cushion of short, fringed yellow petals 1.00   1.50

8.4 **L'Etincelante.** (Dessert, 1905). Very broad petals of the finest bright carmine, broad silvery border, crown or gold stamens at the center; semi-double; superb 1.50   2.00   3.00

7.7 **Lucienne.** (Dessert, 1908). Large, white, single flower, very slightly tinted purple, fading to pure white. Central tuft of golden stamens. Very strong grower and free bloomer. Early midseason.................................. 1.00   1.50

8.5 **Madeline Gauthier.** (Dessert). Single. Rich and fine silvery fleshy pink, exquisite delicately tinted 2.00   2.50

8.5 **Marguerite Dessert.** (Dessert, 1913). Pure white, entirely powdered and splashed with carmine; central tuft of golden stamens; one of the most exquisite varieties. Large single flower; very attractive. Early................... 3.00

	3-5 eye	1 yr.	2 yr.
). (Japan-Barr, 1893). Dark crimson, central tuft of filamentous petals edged crimson and tipped gold. Very choice. Late	2.00	2.50	
r 1001. A very beautiful single Peony, similar in texture and color to Tokio and Ama-no-sode. The yellow stamens form a heavy tuft, like the Japanese Peonies, but do not change their color to correspond with the petals. It is somewhat dwarf and the flowers are a little smaller than those of Tokio....		2.50	
of Langport. (Kelway). Distinct shade of brilliant peach pink, wonderfully beautiful variety	4.50	5.50	
Dawn. (Barr). Large white petals tinged blush, resembling a large water lily	1.00	1.50	
of May. One of the finest single whites	.75		2.00
Wheel. (Japan). Medium sized flower with clear white guards	2.00	3.00	
Ganoko. (Japan). Velvety dark red guards; center golden yellow slightly streaked red	4.00	5.00	
bako. (Japan). Broad petals of clear soft pink, a little darker than Tokio. Very large flower	17.50	20.00	
loor. Single. Rich purple-garnet. Medium size flower; strong grower; free bloomer.	1.00	1.50	
(Jap. Dessert, 1910). Color, old rose; very large, showing a central tuft of golden filamentous petals. Beautiful variety, strong grower, and free bloomer. Very choice. Best all around Jap	4.00	5.00	
ine. (Dessert, 1908). Large cup-shaped flower like a tulip; brilliant red, with velvety reflex	1.50	2.00	
). (Dessert). Bright lively pink, slightly tinted with carmine, central tuft of golden stamens; large flower. Exceedingly beautiful		2.00	
yi Major. Single. Large pure white flowers. Vigorous grower; free bloomer.	1.50	2.00	
(Dessert, 1910). Guard petals pure white, narrow central petals white tinged straw yellow, and tipped with a little carmine point	1.50	2.00	
inatsuki. (Japan). Exceedingly beautiful white Peony with the petaloids tipped with pink	2.00		

e wishing to plant perennial gardens should take up the matter at once, have the ground prepared he plants may be set early in September. If perennials are set late in the fall or in spring, they little bloom the first year. Set early in the fall, they become thoroughly established and give a ount of themselves the following summer.

re always glad to assist our customers in making a selection of Peonies, Phlox, Iris, etc. Please y the results desired, size of plot to be planted, etc.

DON'T OVERLOOK THESE CONVENIENT COLLECTIONS

are four collections, carefully made, regardless of price, to cover all colors, early (E), midseason ate (L) bloom, of varieties anyone might be happy to own. If desired however, substitutes may r the purchaser. Please note low prices for one-year plants, all of which will bloom next year.

LECTION No. 1	3-5 eye Div.	1-Yr.
te and Yellow		
erneville	$ .50	$ .75
(M)	.75	1.00
xlma (M)	.50	.75
sse (L)	.50	.75
oine (L)	.75	1.00
Pink		
ind (E)	.50	.75
rdier (M)	1.00	1.50
s. Gombault (M)	1.00	1.50
usse (L)	.75	1.00
rc (S)	.75	1.00
l (E)	.50	1.00
alhau (L)	.50	.75
Red		
se (M)	.75	1.00
Talindyke (L)	.75	1.00
field (E)	.75	1.00
	$10.25	$14.75
rice	8.50	12.00

COLLECTION No. 2	3-5 eye Div.	1-Yr.
White and Yellow		
La Tendresse (E)	$ .75	$ 1.00
Marcelle Dessert (M)	1.00	1.50
Couronne d'Or (L)	.75	1.00
Baroness Schroeder (M)	1.00	1.50
Pink		
Eugenie Verdier (M)	1.00	1.50
Germaine Bigot (M)	.75	1.25
Alfred de Musset (L)	.75	1.00
Carnea Elegans (L)	.75	1.00
Mme. Calot (E)	.50	.75
Mons. Jules Elie (E)	1.00	1.50
Marguerite Gerard (M)	.75	1.00
Mme. Emile Galle (L)	1.00	1.50
Red		
Mikado, Single (L)	2.00	2.50
Augustin d'Hour (M)	.75	1.00
Adolphe Rousseau (E)	1.50	2.00
	$14.25	$20.00
Net Price	11.50	16.00

LECTION No. 3	3-5 eye Div.	1-Yr.
raine (L)	$ 1.75	$ 2.00
(M)	2.00	3.00
)	1.50	2.00
as (L)	2.50	3.00
)	2.50	3.00
Dessert (L)	2.00	3.00
hardt (M)	1.50	2.00
(M)	2.50	3.50
	$16.25	$21.50
rice	14.50	19.50

COLLECTION No. 4	3-5 eye Div.	1-Yr.
Le Cygne (E)	$ 6.00	$ 8.00
Laura Dessert (M)	4.00	6.00
Solange (L)	2.50	3.50
Jeannot (L)	5.00	6.00
Walter Faxon (M)	3.00	4.00
Rosa Bonheur (M)	2.50	3.50
Martha Bulloch (L)	5.00	6.00
Mons. Martin Cahuzac (E)	2.00	2.50
	$30.00	$39.50
Net Price	27.00	35.00

Japanese Iris

Flowers six to ten inches in diameter; will grow in almost any soil that does not become too dry in summer. Prefer a warm, sunny location.

The best time to plant is July, and from that on until the middle of September the plants may be safely planted in localities not too far north, so that they may have time to establish themselves before cold weather sets in. If they are planted rather late, they should be freely mulched after the ground is frozen in late autumn to keep the ground from heaving.

Make out your order for Japanese Iris and deduct from the total 15% for orders between $10 and $25. For $25 and up, deduct 25%.

Net Price of Mixture: $1.50 per 10; $10 per 100.

3. **Betty Jean Childs.** Single. White faintly splashed and veined with orchid, petaloids deeper shade. 60 cts.; 3 at 55 cts. each.
4. **Catherine Parry.** Double. Blue overlaid with rosy-red. High tufts in center. 40 cts.; 3 or more 35 cts. each.
5. **Koko-No-Iro.** Deep purple suffused with violet, slightly veined with white. Beautiful golden center radiating into lines. Very tall, strong grower, abundant bloomer. 25 cts. each; $2.00 per 10; $15 per 100.
6. **Eleanor Parry.** Double. Claret red, flamed white and blue. Medium size. Very good. 50 cts.; 3 or more at 45 cts. each.
8. **Frances E. Cleveland.** Semi-double. Very large blue flower. 50 cts.; 3 or more at 45 cts. each.
10. **Datedogus.** Single. Very large flowers. Claret red with orange blotches, surrounded by a halo of blue radiating into heavy lines. Standards light claret and white. 50 cts.; 3 or more at 45 cts. each.
11. **Hano-No-Nishiki.** Violet purple veined with white. 25 cts.; 3 or more at 20 cts. each.
12. **Blue Jay.** Double. Sky blue with distinct white lines on each petal. 50 cts.; $4.50 per 10.
14. **Shishi-Ikari.** White ground, veined with dark purple. 30 cts.; $2.50 per 10.
15. **Gekka-No-Nami.** (Syn. Gold Bound). Pure white yellowish blotches; petaloid stigmas; six petals. 50 cents.; 3 or more at 45 cts. each.
16. **Kumo-Ma-No-Sora.** Immense white crepy petals with a delicate sky blue halo overlaying a portion of the petals. 50 cts.; 3 or more 45 cts. each.
40. **Margaret S. Hendrickson.** Triple. Large wavy petals of soft bluish violet. Cast of blue radiating from white center. $1.00 each.
43. **Purple,** overlaid with navy blue, two standards; petaloid stigmas purple and blue; large orange blotches; six petals. Late. 40 cts.; 3 or more at 35 cts. each.
44. **Amethyst.** Single. Very large, wavy petals, most exquisite lavender shade. 50 cts.; 3 or more at 45 cts. each.
45. **Mahogany.** Double. Dark red, shaded maroon. 60 cts.; 3 or more at 50 cts. each.
46. **Norma.** Double. Exquisite silky lavender-pink, with clear blue halo surrounding the yellow blotch at base of petals. Fine and large. 40 cts.; 3 or more at 35 cts. each.
49. **Red Riding Hood.** Single. Fine amarinth veined and suffused white. 40 cts.; 3 or more at 35 cts. each.
51. **Sho-Jo.** White, heavily veined violet; three small petals, violet with white border. 40 cts.; 3 or more at 35 cts. each.
53. **Azure.** Double. Immense flower, exquisitely wavy, mauve-blue, with darker halo surrounding the blotches at the throat of the lower petals. 40 cts.; 3 or more at 35 cts. each.
54. **Sufo-No-Koi.** Double. Color blotched and speckled blue and white with yellow throat; stamens lavender tipped blue. 40 cts.; 3 or more at 35 cts. each.
55. **Blue Bird.** Single. Deep velvet blue. 50 cts.; 3 or more at 45 cts. each.
56. **Kumo-No-Obi.** Double. Sky blue petals lined with white. 40 cts.; 3 or more at 35 cts. each.
58. **Nomo-opi-notaki.** Double. Bright crimson; white halo surrounding yellow blotches; petaloids light violet. 40 cts. each; 3 or more at 35 cts. each.
65. **Ho-Ojo.** Ruddy crimson, primrose blotches, with white halo; petaloid stigmas white, tipped with purple; six petals. 40 cts.; 3 or more at 35 cts. each.

JAPANESE IRIS

67. **White,** medium height; three large petals; three small petals; late. 40 cts.; 3 or more at 35 cts. each.
71. **Pyramid.** Double. Dark violet blue, slightly veined white; very fine. Last to bloom. 25 cts.; 3 or more at 20 cts.; $15 per 100.
72. **Double,** rich deep purple with yellow blotches. 25 cts.; 3 or more at 20 cts. each.
74. **Pink Progress.** Single. Ashy-grey lavender; clear blue halo overlaid with silver sheen. 40 cts.; 3 or more at 35 cts. each.
75. **Kamata.** Single. Deepest sky-blue, veined white, very distinct. 40 cts.; 3 or more at 35 cts. each.
76. **Mirage.** Single. Light pink, suffused with light blue towards the center. 30 cts.; 3 or more at 25 cts. each.
80. **Alida Lovett.** Double. Very heavily veined lavender blue on a white ground. 75 cts. each; 3 for $2.00.
82. **Templeton.** Double. Light violet, mottled pink and white. 50 cts.; 3 or more at 45 cts. each.
98. **Totty's True Blue.** Double. Dark violet blue. 60 cts.; 3 or more at 55 cts. each.
100. **Ruffled Monster.** Double, deep pinkish plum, heavily veined white surrounding the yellow blotch, finely formed and beautiful, ruffled, very large and striking. 75 cts. each; 3 for $2.00.

VARIOUS IRISES

Sibirica. (Siberian Flag). Two to three feet high, with narrow, grassy leaves; showy blue flowers, beautifully veined with white and violet. 20 cts.; $1.50 per ten.

Siberica Emperor. Dark violet blue. Largest blooms of any of the Sibericans. 60 cts.; $5.00 per 10.

Siberica Perry's Blue. A large flower of clear blue with horizontal falls, probably the finest Siberican Iris; very scarce. 60 cts.; $5.00 per 10.

Oriental Siberican Snow Queen. Found by Mr. Barr in Japan. Pure, glistening white with yellow throat. 42 inches in height. 25 cts.; $2.00 per 10.

Pumila. In addition to making fine edgings for borders, this species and its varieties are excellent for rock gardens. They are very dwarf and bloom very early. 25 cts.; $2.00 per 10.

Pumila Lutea. S and F splendid yellow.

Pumila Bride. Ivory white.

Pumila Cyanea. Beautiful deep blue.

Cristata. Crested Iris. A gem for rock garden. 25 cts.

S. G. HARRIS, TARRYTOWN, N. Y.

The use of this **Order Sheet** will insure the
prompt and correct filling of your order
of not less than $3.00

Date sent ....

	Please Do Not Write Here
Name	
City	No.
Street ....State...................	Rec'd.
Express Address (if different from P. O.)...............................	
	Shipped
Via	
Ship about....................1928	AMOUNT ENCLOSED
	By

Quantity	DOUBLE VARIETIES	3-5 Eye Div.	1-Yr.	2-Yr. $	
	ADOLPHE ROUSSEAU	$1.50	$2.00		
	ALBA SULPHUREA	.75	1.00	1.50	
	ALBATRE	.75	1.00	1.50	
	ALBERT CROUSSE	.75	1.00	1.50	
	ALFRED DE MUSSET	.75	1.00	1.50	
	ALSACE-LORRAINE	1.75	2.00		
	ARMANDINE MECHIN	.50	.75	1.00	
	ASA GRAY	1.00	1.25	2.00	
	AUGUSTIN D'HOUR	.75	1.00	1.50	
	AURORE	.75	1.00	1.50	
	AVALANCHE	.75	1.00	1.50	
	BARONESS SCHROEDER	1.00	1.50	2.25	
	BOULE DE NEIGE	.50	.75	1.25	
	CANARI	.50	.75		
	CARNEA ELEGANS	.75	1.00		
	CHERRY HILL	3.50	4.50		
	CLAIRE DUBOIS	1.00	1.25	2.00	
	COURONNE D'OR	.75	1.00	1.50	
	DE CANDOLLE	.50	.75	1.25	
	DELACHEI	.75	1.00		
	DORCHESTER	.75		1.25	
	DOCTEUR BRETONNEAU (Guerin)	.50			
	DUC DE WELLINGTON	.50	.75		
	DUCHESS DE NEMOURS	.50	.75		
	EDULIS SUPERBA	.50	.75	1.25	
	ELWOOD PLEAS	2.50	3.00		
	EUGENE BIGOT	1.50	2.00		
	EUGENE VERDIER	1.50	2.00	3.00	
	EUGENIE VERDIER	1.00			
	FELIX CROUSSE	.75	1.00	1.50	
	FESTIVA	.50	.75	1.00	
	FESTIVA MAXIMA	.50	.75	1.25	
	FRANCES WILLARD	1.50	2.00		
	GALATHEE	3.00	3.50		
	GENERAL BERTRAND	.50	.75	1.00	
	GERMAINE BIGOT	.75	1.25	2.00	
	GISMONDA	1.00	1.50	2.00	
	GLOIRE DE CHAS. GOMBAULT	1.00	1.50	2.00	
	For Discounts and Special Offer, See Page 5.				

Quantity		3-5 Eye Div.	1-Yr.	2-Yr. $
	GRANDIFLORA	$ .75	$1.00	2.00
	GRANDIFLORA NIVEA PLENA	.50	.75	1.00
	HENRY AVERY	3.00	3.50	
	JAMES KELWAY	1.00	1.50	2.25
	JEANNE D'ARC	.75	1.00	1.50
	JEANNOT	5.00	6.00	
	JUBILEE	1.50	2.00	3.00
	KARL ROSENFIELD	.75	1.00	1.50
	KELWAY'S GLORIOUS	8.00	10.00	
	LADY ALEXANDRA DUFF	2.00	2.50	
	LA FIANCEE	.75		
	LA FRANCE	3.00	4.00	
	LA LORRAINE	5.00		
	LAMARTINE	.75	1.50	2.25
	LA PERLE		1.00	
	LA ROSIERE	.75	1.00	
	LA TENDRESSE	.75	1.00	1.50
	LAURA DESSERT	4.00		
	LE CYGNE	7.00	9.00	
	LIVINGSTONE	.75	1.00	
	LONGFELLOW	2.50	3.50	
	LORD KITCHENER		1.50	
	MME. AUGUSTE DESSERT	1.00	1.50	
	MME. BOLLET	.50	.75	1.00
	MME. BUCQUET	.75	1.00	1.50
	MME. CHAUMY	.50	.75	1.00
	MME. CALOT	.50	.75	1.00
	MME. CROUSSE	.50	.75	1.00
	MME. DE GALHOU	.50	.75	1.00
	MME. DE VATRY	.50	.75	1.00
	MME. DE VERNEVILLE	.50	.75	1.00
	MME. DUCEL	.50	1.00	1.50
	MME. EMILE GALLE	1.00	1.50	
	MME. EMILE LEMOINE	1.00	1.50	
	MME. JULES DESSERT	2.00	3.00	
	MME. LEMONIER	.75	1.00	1.50
	MME. GAUDICHAU	2.50	3.50	
	MME. REIGNOUX	.75		1.25
	MLLE. LEONIE CALOT	.75	1.00	1.50
	MLLE. MARIE CALOT	.50	.75	1.00
	MLLE. ROUSSEAU	.75		1.50
	MARCELLE DESSERT	1.00	1.50	2.00
	MARGUERITE GERARD	.75	1.00	1.50
	MARIE CROUSSE	1.00	1.50	2.00
	MARIE JACQUIN	.75	1.00	1.50
	MARIE LEMOINE	.75	1.00	1.50
	MARTHA BULLOCH	5.00	6.00	
	MARY WOODBURY SHAYLOR	5.00	6.00	
	MILTON HILL	3.00	4.00	5.00
	MODESTE GUERIN	.75		
	MONS. DUPONT	.75		
	MONS. JULES ELIE	1.00	1.50	2.00
	MONS. MARTIN CAHUZAC	2.00	2.50	
	MRS. EDWARD HARDING	12.00		

Quantity		3-5 Eye Div.	1-Yr.	2-Yr. $
	NUMBER ONE	1.00	1.50	2.25
	OCTAVIE DEMAY	.75	1.00	1.50
	OFFICINALIS RUBRA	.75	1.00	1.50
	PETITE RENEE	1.00	1.50	2.25
	PHILOMELE	.75	1.00	1.50
	PHILLIPE RIVOIRE	7.50		
	PIERRE DESSERT			
	PIERRE DUCHARTRE	.75	1.00	
	PRIMEVERE	2.00	3.00	4.00
	PRINCE DE TALINDYKE	.75	1.00	
	RAOUL DESSERT	5.00	6.00	
	RAPHAEL	.75	1.00	
	REINE HORTENSE	1.00	1.50	2.00
	RICHARD CARVEL	3.00	4.00	
	ROSA BONHEUR	2.50	3.50	4.00
	RUBRA SUPERBA	.75	1.00	
	SARAH BERNHARDT	1.50	2.00	3.00
	SOLANGE	2.50	3.50	
	SOUV. DE LOUIS BIGOT	3.50	4.50	
	THERESE	2.50	3.00	4.50
	TOURANGELLE	2.00	2.50	
		.50	.75	1.25
		.50	.75	
		.75	1.00	
		.50	.75	
		3.00	4.00	

ESE VARIETIES

Quantity		3-5 Eye Div.	1-Yr.	2-Yr. $
		8.00	10.00	
		2.00	2.50	
	EGLANTINE			
	EMILY	1.00	1.50	
	FESTIVA FRAGRANS			
	FUYAJO	6.00	7.00	
	HERMES	.50	.75	
	ISANI-GIDUI	8.00	10.00	
		1.50	2.00	
	LA FIANCEE	1.75	2.25	
	LE JOUR	3.50	4.50	
	L'ETINCELANTE	1.50	2.00	3.00
	LEMON QUEEN	1.00	1.50	
	LUCIENNE	1.00	1.50	
	MARGUERITE DESSERT	3.00		
	MIKADO	2.00	2.50	
	MADELINE GAUTHIER	2.00	2.50	
	NUMBER 1001		2.50	
	PRIDE OF LANGPORT	4.50	5.50	
	QUEEN OF MAY	.75		2.00
	ROSY DAWN	1.00	1.50	
	SNOW WHEEL	2.00	3.00	
	SOME GANOKO	4.00	5.00	
	TAMATBAKO	17.50	20.00	
	THE MOOR	1.00	1.50	
	TOKIO	4.00	5.00	
	VELOUTINE	1.50	2.00	
	VENISE			
	WHITLEYI MAJOR	1.50	2.00	
		1.50	2.00	
	YOUCHINATSUKI			

Quantity	OTHER PLANTS	$	

A PART OF OUR BEARDED IRIS

German Iris has never been more sive, and I know of no place where the large growing varieties, in the articularly, are offered at such a rieties as Pallida Speciosa, three to

blooms you would like to produce, it is profitable to work into it some bonemeal before planting and to give a light annual dressing, but it is safest to use no other fertilizer of any kind.

The following abbreviations are used: S means

7.8. **Eldorado.** S fiery opalescent; F old gold silhouetted with purple, a totally distinct harmony of striking hues, perfectly blended. Has weak stems. 30 in. 35 cts.; 3 for 85 cts.; 10 for $2.50.

8.0. **Fairy.** White, delicately bordered and suffused soft blue. Very fragrant. 30 in. 25 cts.; 3 for 50 cts.; 10 for $1.50.

7.6. **Florentina Alba.** Creamy-white, faintly flushed lavender; the blooms are quite fragrant. 2 feet. 25 cts.; 3 for 50 cts.; 10 for $1.50.

6.1. **Gracchus.** S lemon yellow, with tinge of primrose; F nearly crimson with red purple tracings. Early. 25 cts.; 3 for 60 cts.; 10 for $1.50.

7.7. **Ingeborg.** Pure white. Large flowers of handsome form. 25 cts.; 3 for 60 cts.; 10 for $1.50.

7.9. **Iris King.** S old gold; F very large velvety maroon, edged with gold. Well named "The King of the Iris." 28 in. 35 cts.; 3 for 70 cts.; 10 for $2.00.

8.0. **Jacquesiana.** S bright coppery crimson; F rich maroon; very handsome. Scarce. 30 in. 35 cts.; 3 for 85 cts.; 10 for $2.50.

7.3. **Jeanne d'Arc.** S white, penciled lilac; F white bordered lilac at base. 25 cts.; 3 for 60 cts.; 10 for $1.50.

7.4. **Kharput.** S violet; F velvety purple. Very large handsome flower. 30 inches. 25 cts.; 3 for 60 cts.; 10 for $1.50.

7.8. **Kochii.** (Syn Atropurpurea). S and F rich claret-purple. Often sold under the name of Black Prince. 15 inches. 25 cts.; 3 for 60 cts.; 10 for $1.50.

9.0. **Lent A. Williamson.** S lavender violet; F velvety royal purple. A massive flower of high standard. 50 cts.; 3 for $1.25.

9.1. **Lord of June.** S light chickory blue; F lavender violet. Said to be one of the world's finest Irises. 50 cts.; 3 for $1.25.

7.9. **Loreley.** S light yellow; F ultra marine, bordered with cream. 28 inches. 25 cts.; 3 for 50 cts.; 10 for $1.50.

7.4. **Madame Chereau.** White elegantly frilled with a wide border of clear blue; one of the most beautiful. 31 inches. 25 cts.; 3 for 50 cts.; 10 for $1.50.

8.1. **Ma Mie.** S pure white, frilled light violet; F white, penciled and margined lavender and veined green. Beautiful and compact. 35 cts.; 3 for 85 cts.; 10 for $2.50.

7.8. **Mary Garden.** S pale yellow flushed pale lavender; F creamy white minutely dotted and veined maroon; stigma clear yellow. An elegant flower of distinct iridescent effect. 28 inches. 35 cts.; 3 for 85 cts.; 10 for $2.50.

Mary Orth. S light blue violet; F dark blue violet. One of Farr's best. 24 in. $1.00; 3 for $2.50.

Mildred Presby. S white; F rich dark purple. Very choice, best of its type. 30 in. $2.00; 3 for $5.00.

8.4. **Monsignor.** S rich satiny violet; F velvety purple crimson with lighter margin. Large flowers. Very late. Beautiful. 2 ft. 25 cts.; 3 for 50 cts.; 10 for $1.50.

Mother of Pearl. S and F pale bluish lavender with a faint creamy undertone. Large flowers with a cluster and iridescent similar to the lining of the sea shell. 40 in. 50 cts.; 3 for $1.25.

6.8. **Mrs. H. Darwin.** 30 in. Late. S pure white; F white, finely reticulated. One of the most charming whites. 25 cts.; 3 for 60 cts.; 10 for $1.50.

6.8. **Mrs. Neubrunner.** Deep golden-yellow; darker than Aurea. 25 cts.; 3 for 60 cts.; 10 for $1.50.

7.3. **Nibelungen.** S fawn-yellow; F violet purple on bronze. Very large. 25 cts.; 3 for 60 cts.; 10 for $1.50.

8.1. **Parc de Neuilly.** S and F very dark navy-blue of reddish tinge. Large flowers of perfect form. 35 cts.; 3 for 85 cts.; 10 for $2.50.

7.9. **Parisiana.** S deep lavender, with some white on the inner side; F white beautifully lined and tinted with lavender, matching the standards. 35 cts.; 3 for 85 cts.; 10 for $2.50.

7.8. **Perfection.** S light lavender; F velvety black violet. Very rich and distinctive flowers. 25 cts.; 3 for 60 cts.; 10 for $1.50.

7.7. **Pocahontas.** Pure white, faintly bordered pale blue. 35 cts.; 3 for 85 cts.; 10 for $2.50.

8.3. **Prosper Laugier.** S light bronze-red; F velvety ruby-purple, with orange beard. Very handsome. 35 cts.; 3 for 85 cts.; 10 for $2.50.

8.4. **Quaker Lady.** S smoky lavender with yellow shadings; F ageratim-blue and old gold, with Its distinguishing name is most suitable. 38 in. 35 cts.; 3 for 60 cts.; 10 for $1.50.

7.5. **Queen Alexandra.** S fawn, shot with lilac; F lilac, reticulated bronze at base. Beard yellow. Very beautiful. 30 inches. 25 cts.; 3 for 60 cts.; 10 for $1.50.

9.0. **Queen Caterina.** Pale lavender with smooth, iridescent sheen; strong, erect stems. Free and reliable bloomer. One of the finest Iris. 75 cts. each; 3 for $2.00.

8.4. **Rhein Nixe.** S pure white; F deep violet blue, with a white edge. A great favorite. Equal to many of the newer introductions. 3 feet. 35 cts.; 3 for 85 cts.; 10 for $2.50.

6.9. **Rose Unique.** Bright violet rose. Nearest approach to a pink Iris. Early. 35 cts.; 3 for 70 cts.; 10 for $2.50.

8.3. **Seminole.** S white; F white, faintly shaded blue with network of blue lines. Vigorous grower. 50 cts. each; 3 for $1.25.

9.3. **Souvenir de Mme. Gaudichau.** Very large deep purple bicolor. Rich velvety petals. S broad, violet; F drooping brilliant velvety blackish purple. Over 3 feet. $1.00; 3 for $2.50.

8.8. **Shekinah.** The first good yellow of Pallida type and growth. Good size, graceful flower with both S and F pinard-yellow. Vigorous plant with high and widely branched stalks. 3 feet. 50 cts.; 3 for $1.00.

6.5. **Victorine.** S mottled blue; F violet blue, mottled white. 27 in. 25 cts.; 3 for 50 cts.; 10 for $1.50.

7.3. **Windham.** S delicate lilac; F white striped with lavender. Much of the appearance of Her Majesty. Good "pink." 24 in. 25 cts.; 3 for 60 cts.; 10 for $1.50.

7.2. **Wyomissing.** S creamy white suffused delicate soft rose; F deep rose base, shading to flesh-colored border. 35 cts.; 3 for 70 cts.; 10 for $2.50.

7.5. **Zua.** S and F white, slightly tinged lilac; texture like heavily frosted crepe, with edges crimpled and crinkled, immense flowers, free bloomer. Very fragrant. 50 cts.; 3 for $1.25; 10 for $3.50.

PALLIDA SECTION

7.9. **Albert Victor.** S soft blue; F beautiful lavender; large and fine. 40 inches. 25 cts.; 3 for 60 cts.; 10 for $1.50.

8.8. **Dalmatica.** S lavender; F clear deep lavender; flowers very large, extra fine. A grand variety for massing and for cut flowers. 40 inches. 35 cts.; 3 for 85 cts.; 10 for $2.50.

5.0. **Garibaldi.** Similar to Her Majesty, but deeper pink. 25 cts.; 3 for 60 cts.; 10 for $1.50.

7.3. **Her Majesty.** S rose-pink; F bright crimson, tinged a darker shade. 35 cts.; 3 for 70 cts.; 10 for $2.00.

8.1. **Juniata.** S and F clear blue, deeper than Dalmatica. Tallest of all the bearded Irises; foliage long and drooping; flowers large and fragrant. 35 cts.; 3 for 60 cts.; 10 for $1.50.

8.2. **Lohengrin** (Pallida). S and F soft silvery-mauve, shading nearly to white at the claw. 33 inches. 30 cts.; 3 for 75 cts.; 10 for $2.00.

8.0. **Powhatan.** S light bishop-violet with deeper border; F deep purple shaded crimson; large, horizontal spreading flower. 50 cts.; 3 for $1.25.

6.3. **Speciosa.** S dark lavender, shaded lighter; F lavender, shaded bright purple. 42 inches. 25 cts.; 3 for 60 cts.; 10 for $1.50.

A plant ready for planting consists of 3 essential parts—the leaves, the rhizome (often mistakenly called bulb), and the roots. Drying does not injure the leaves or rhizomes, but kills the roots. See that they do not dry out; if the soil is dry at planting time, fill the trench or hole with water and after it has soaked into the ground, spread the roots over the moist surface and draw soil over them, tramping it down firmly and covering with loose soil. The rhizome should be just below or at the surface and should be held firmly in place if the soil has been properly packed over the roots.

y flower garden or per-nnial border? Use plenty of Peonies, Iris and
uous bloom from May 15 to October 15; first, the bearded Iris, May and
es in June, Japanese I-is in July and Phlox, July, August and September.
r be used colonies of Aquilegia, Digitalis, Delphinium and other favorites
s to suit ones taste.

PHLOX

es in time of bloom,
n popularity, are the
have weeded out all
believe that our list
iny firm.
each; **$2.50 per ten;**
.00 per ten. Five at
in five of a kind are

Our spring, 1928 catalog listing choicest varieties of fruit and ornamental trees, shrubs and
flowering Evergreens and many cultural directions
for the planter will be sent on application.

lox

nts and should there-
han most other plant-
onserve the moisture,
i soil like Peonies and
ar the roots. A little
ace of the ground be-
, but be careful not

crimson center.

;ht salmon-pink, with

ad eye; one of the
· per ten. Blooming

crimson-carmine eye;
·s very large; sturdy,

ite.

with crimson eye.

fully six weeks earlier

itinues in bloom three

ety, which should be

blush pink; strong
with petals of great

p rose center; rather
· Superb.

ie best. Tall.

on pink.

ox, resembling Pan-
r heads; a soft clear
ng grower.

ed; crimson eye.

bright crimson.

lovely shade of deep
rerlaid with a scarlet

ndividual flowers very

HARDY PERENNIALS

All our Perennials are strong field grown; please
note that with the exception of the Iris and Peonies,
we are offering Perennials in quantities of three instead of singly. As it takes little longer to label
and wrap three of a kind instead of one, I believe
we could handle small quantities at the present
prices without a loss. Owing to the very favorable
season all our Perennials have done exceedingly well
and the sizes will run larger than our usual large·
sizes.

5 plants of a kind will be priced at the 10 rate.

Make out your order for these Perennials and
deduct 20%, our removal sale discount.

Astilbe (Spiraea).	3	10
Ordinary size ....$	.90	$2.50
XX	1.25	3.50
XXX	1.50	4.50

Queen Alexandra (Pink).
Peach Blossom (Pink).
Palmata (Tall), (Pink).
Gladstone (White).
Floribunda (White).

Convallaria (Lily of the Valley).		
Heavy Clumps	1.25	3.50
Ordinary Clumps	.90	2.50
Hibiscus (Mallow Marvels).......	.90	2.50
Hemerocallis (Yellow Day Lily)......	.90	2.50

Aurantiaca Major (June).
Flava (May).
Kwanso-Double (July).
Thunbergii-Lemon Lily (July).

Hosta (Funkia), XX...............	.90	2.50

Yucca (Adam's Needle).		
Ordinary size	.75	2.00
XX	1.25	3.00

Reduced Prices of Roses *for* Fall, 1928

We are glad to be able to offer our usual list of varieties of Hybrid Perpetuals, Hybrid Teas, and climbing roses at considerably reduced prices and assure our customers as fine stock as we have ever offered. In case customers prefer spring shipment, we will book the order at fall prices, provided a deposit of one-quarter the amount of the order is made this fall. These roses, grown on the Japanese Multiflora, now considered by rosarians the best stock, are sure to give abundant bloom with very little trouble. ·Late November shipment for all, except Hybrid Teas, for which we advise early spring shipment north of New York.

A combination of rates may be applied in one order.

Varieties offered at 55c, $4.00 per 10, $35.00 per 100.

Varieties offered at 70c, $6.00 per 10, $55.00 per 100.

Varieties offered at $1.00, $9.00 per ten.

Orders for 50 or more plants, not less than 3 of a name, 100 rate.

Orders for 6 to 50 plants, not less than 3 of a name, 10 rate.

Less than 3 of a name will be sold at single rate.

HYBRID TEA

Betty. Ruddy gold. 70 cts.
Columbia. Glowing pink. 70 cts.
Eldorado. Beautiful golden yellow. 70 cts.
E. P. H. Kingma. Semi-double. Orange yellow. 70 cts.
Etoile de France. Velvety crimson. 70 cts.
Francis Scott Key. Crimson red. 70 cts.
Grange Colombe. Soft ivory white. 70 cts.
Gruss an Teplitz. Brilliant scarlet. 70 cts.
Imperial Potentate. Dark, shining rose pink. 70 cts.
Killarney Queen. Flesh suffused pale pink. 70 cts.
Lady Alice Stanley. Deep coral red. 70 cts.
Lady Ashtown. Soft medium shade of pink .70 cts.
Lady Pirrie. ·Coppery salmon. 70 cts.
Laurent Carle. Brilliant velvety carmine. 70 cts.
Los Angeles. Pink. 70 cts.
Mme. Butterfly. Pink. 70 cts.
Mme. C. Testout. Pink. 70 cts.
Mme. E. Herriot. Terra cotta. 70 cts.
Mme. Jules Bouche. White. 70 cts.
Miss Lolita Armour. Coral red. 70 cts.
Mrs. Aaron Ward. Indian yellow. 70 cts.
Mrs. A. R. Waddell. Orange and salmon. ·70 cts.
Mrs. Henry Morse. Contrasting toned pink, yellow glow. 70 cts.
Mrs. W. C. Egan. Deep flesh color with golden glow. 70 cts.
Ophelia. Salmon. 70 cts.
Padre. Coppery scarlet. 70 cts.
Queen of Fragrance. Shell pink. 70 cts.
Radiance. Even shade of pink. 70 cts.
Red Radiance. Cerise red. 70 cts.
Rev. F. Page Roberts. Orange gold, shading to saffron yellow. $1.50.
Souvenir de Claudius Pernet. Lovely sunflower yellow. 70 cts.
Souvenir de Georges Pernet. Brick red. 70 cts.
William F. Dreer. Shell pink, golden yellow at base of petals. 70 cts.

HYBRID PERPETUAL

Frau Karl Druschki. White. 70 cts.
George Arends. Pink. 70 cts.
Mrs. John Laing. Pink. 70 cts.
Paul Neyron. Pink. 70 cts.
Prince Camille de Rohan. Crimson. 70 cts.
Ulrich Brunner. Scarlet. 70 cts.

CLIMBING ROSES

Prices—2-yr., 55 cts.

American Beauty. Beautiful rose of medium pink. 4-yr., $1.00.
American Pillar. Single, lovely shade of pink. 4-yr., $1.00.
Bess Lovett. Clear, bright red.
Dr. Huey. Deepest crimson-maroon.
Dr. W. Van Fleet. Rich flesh pink.
Dorothy Perkins. Pink.
Emily Gray. Beautiful orange yellow.
Gardenia. Semi-double, yellow.
Hiawatha. Single, crimson.
Lady Gay. Delicate cherry pink.
Mary Wallace. Bright pink, shading to salmon. 4-yr., $1.00.
Paul's Scarlet. Semi-double, vivid scarlet.
Setigera. Single, pink.
Silver Moon. White.

MISCELLANEOUS ROSES

Crested Moss. Deep pink. 70 cts.; 3-yr., $1.00.
Edith Cavell. Brilliant crimson. 4-yr. old, $1.00.
Ideal. Scarlet. 4-yr. old, $1.00.
Persian Yellow. Small bright yellow. 75 cts.
Rosa Hugonis. Single yellow. 70 cts.; 4-yr., $1.50.
Salet Moss. Rose pink. 70 cts.; 3-yr., $1.00.

RUGOSA

3-year heavy. 70 cts.

Belle Poitevine. Semi-double, clear pink.
Blanc Double de Coubert. Double white.
New Century. Flesh pink.
Nova Zembla. White.
Rugosa Alba. Single white.
Rugosa Rubra. Rosy crimson.

My dear Mr. Harris:—

Also I want to tell you that all the roses you sent me have bloomed fully, and those you sent to Scotland also.

(Signed) ANNE H. PATTESON

CPSIA information can be obtained
at www.ICGtesting.com
Printed in the USA
LVHW05s1451051018
592550LV00009B/579/P